Learning Musical Instruments

Should I Play the
Drums?

Tom Crask

Heinemann Library
Chicago, Illinois

Customer Service 888-454-2279
Visit our website at www.heinemannraintree.com

Designed by Richard Parker and Manhattan Design
Illustrations by Jeff Edwards
Printed and bound in China by Leo Paper Group

11 10 09 08 07
10 9 8 7 6 5 4 3 2 1

Library of Congress Cataloging-in-Publication Data
Crask, Tom.
  Should I play the drums? / Tom Crask.
     p. cm. -- (Learning musical instruments)
  Includes bibliographical references (p.   ), discography, and index.
  ISBN 1-4034-8186-5 (library binding - hardcover)
  1. Drum--Juvenile literature. I. Title. II. Series.
  ML1035.C73 2006
  786.9--dc22   2006006670

Acknowledgments
The publishers would like to thank the following for permission to reproduce photos:
Alamy pp. 4 (Janine Wiedel Photolibrary), 5 Danita Delimont, 18 (Lebrecht Music and Arts Photo Library), 27 (Stockbyte); Corbis pp. 6 (Paul Funston/Gallo Images), 7, 14 (Neal Preston), 15 (Roger Ressmeyer), 21 (Anne Ryan/NewSport), 24 (Kipa/Pugnet Francois); Getty Images pp. 10 (Entertainment), 17 (Photodisc), 22 (Hulton Archive), 23 (Image Bank); Harcourt Education Ltd pp. 8 (Trevor Clifford), 11 (Tudor Photography), 12 (Tudor Photography), 25 (Tudor Photography); Lebrecht p. 16 (David Gee); Photo Edit p. 20 (Tony Freeman); Redferns p. 19 (Peter Stil); Yamaha-Kemble Music (UK) Ltd p. 9.

Cover image of drummer reproduced with permission of Redferns.

The publishers would like to thank Teryl Dobbs for her assistance in the preparation of this book.

Contents

Any words appearing in the text in bold, **like this**, are explained in the Glossary.

Why Do People Play Musical Instruments?

People have made music for thousands of years. It is almost second nature for us to create music by singing or by playing a musical instrument. Creating music is both an art form and entertainment. It can change our moods and emotions and communicate ideas to us without the need for words.

Rhythm is a very important part of any piece of music. In this book you will find out about creating rhythm by playing the drums. You will find out what a drum is, about the history of drumming, and about the different types of drums you can play. Different types of drums are found around the world.

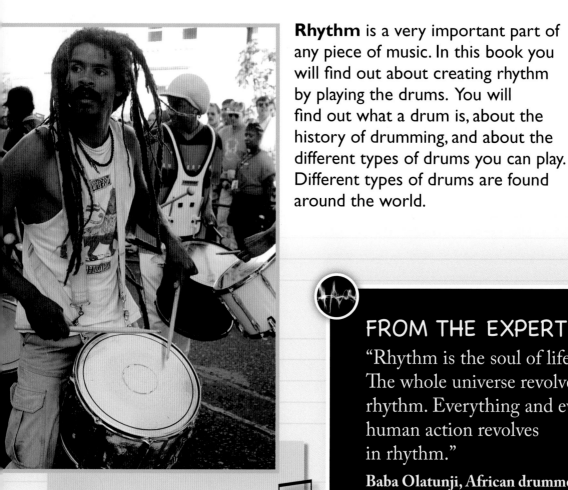

Music is fun to watch and even more fun to play!

FROM THE EXPERTS

"Rhythm is the soul of life. The whole universe revolves in rhythm. Everything and every human action revolves in rhythm."

Baba Olatunji, African drummer

"A good drummer listens as much as he plays."

Indian proverb

A drummer keeps the other musicians playing together and helps make sure that nobody speeds up or slows down.

Choosing your style

One of the great things about the drums is that they are relatively easy to learn. With a little practice, you will be able to play a basic beat within a few hours. Within a few months, you will be able to play along to your favorite songs.

Drums can be played in a wide variety of styles, from **classical** and **jazz** to rock and pop. They can even be played alongside other **percussion instruments**. But first, there are some basic things that every drummer should know.

What Are Drums?

Drums come in many different shapes and sizes, but they all have some features in common. A drum is basically a cylinder with a **membrane**, called the drum **head**, stretched across its open end. Striking the drum on the drum head produces a tone. The cylindrical part of the drum is known as the **shell**.

Almost every culture in the world plays some form of drum. This is an African "talking" drum, played by a Shangaan drummer.

The history of drumming

If the human voice is the oldest instrument in the world, drums are a close second. This is not so surprising when you think that drums are quite simple instruments. All you need to make a drum is a stick and a surface to hit. The oldest drums found date back over 6,000 years.

Drums were once used to communicate. A person's voice does not carry very far, but drums can be heard for many miles. Drums were also used for religious purposes. People believed that they were home to powerful spirits. Only certain people were allowed to touch them.

When the ancient Greeks and Romans arrived in Africa, they started using African drums to keep soldiers marching in pace and to call out orders. They were even used in battle to scare enemies. Many European armies continued this tradition of using drums when they marched.

When African slaves were taken to the Americas in the 1500s, they brought their knowledge of drums with them. Drums also played an important part in Native American and South American cultures.

The modern drum set

By the 1920s, musicians began to play more than one drum at the same time. Once the drums were arranged properly, bands did not need a group of drummers anymore. Bit by bit, the modern drum set took shape.

The **electronic drum** set was developed in the 1980s, after instruments such as the electric piano became popular.

This is the drum corps of the 93rd New York Infantry Regiment in August 1863. Drummers were used by many regiments during the Civil War.

Around the drum set

Modern drum sets include several different types of drum, so that the drummer can produce different sounds. The basic drum set is referred to as a "five-piece" set. There are actually more than five pieces. The "five" just refers to the number of shells. Although the drum set's size can change from drummer to drummer, these are the basic ingredients that every drum set should have:

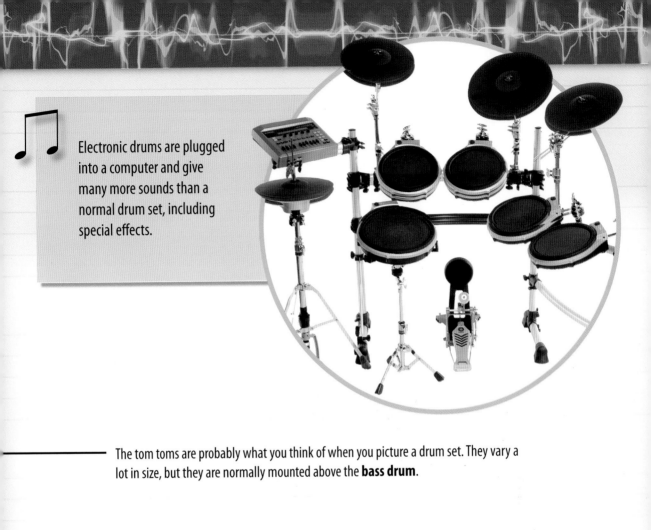

Electronic drums are plugged into a computer and give many more sounds than a normal drum set, including special effects.

The tom toms are probably what you think of when you picture a drum set. They vary a lot in size, but they are normally mounted above the **bass drum**.

The floor toms are mounted on legs. They have a deeper tone than small toms.

The **snare drum**, along with the bass drum, is the center of any drum set and forms the basis for most **rhythms**. It can be made of either wood or steel, and there are various sizes. A snare drum has one major difference from other drums. It has a series of wire springs stretched across its underside. These are what give the snare its distinct sound.

The bass drum is the biggest drum in the set, and it has the deepest tone. Unlike other drums, it rests on its side. It has short legs that lift the drum slightly off the floor. The drummer attaches the tom toms and cymbals to this "platform." The bass drum is not played by hand. Instead, the drummer uses a **beater** connected to a foot pedal.

Other drums

Not all drummers play a five-piece set. There are many different types of drums. Here are some drums that you are likely to see being played or that you may even get to try yourself:

Timpani, or kettle drums, are large orchestral drums used in **classical** music. They are made out of a large copper bowl with a calfskin or plastic head. Timpani are played with felt-tipped mallets and make a specific **pitch** that depends on the drum's size. This pitch can be **tuned** by using a set of pedals around the base of the drum.

Marching drums are normal drums that have been **modified** with a strap or harness so that they can be played while moving. There are many different types of marching drum, although the most common are the marching bass drum, the marching toms, and the marching snare drum.

In different parts of the world, the appearance of drums varies. How they are played also differs. These conga drums are played with the hands.

10

sticks

multi-rods

brushes

Beaters

Beaters are the most important items a drummer can have. Without them, the drummer would have nothing to hit the drums with. Here are some of the different types of beater:

• Sticks come in a variety of lengths and weights. Most drummers have a favorite type. For softer music, such as **jazz**, a light pair of sticks is more suitable. For louder music, heavier sticks are best.

• Brushes have a rubber or plastic handle attached to plastic or steel wires. The length of the wires is usually adjustable. Brushes give a more delicate sound than sticks, especially on cymbals.

• Multi-rods are tightly bound bunches of wooden rods. They are quiet, but not as quiet as wire brushes. They are not as long-lasting as sticks.

• Some mallets have wooden heads, while others have padded heads. They are especially useful for playing drum **rolls** or cymbal rolls. Mallets are mostly used by timpani players. They are also used to play other **percussion instruments** such as bells, xylophones, and marimba.

Different types of beater can be used for different types of music.

How Do Drums Make Their Sound?

A drum is a cylinder (**shell**), with a **membrane** at one or both ends (the drum **head**). When something strikes the drum head, it produces **vibrations** in the air inside the shell. These vibrations make invisible ripples of air. Our brains interpret these movements of air as sound.

Different types of head and different shapes of shell give different shapes to the vibrations inside the drum. We hear these as different **pitches** when the drum is played. A smaller shell creates a higher-pitched sound, while a larger shell creates a deeper sound.

The **snare drum's** distinctive sound comes from the wires underneath (pictured here upside down).

DRUM FACTS: The longest and loudest

The longest drumming marathon was played by Arulanantham Suresh Joachim from Australia. In 2004 he played a set of drums continuously for 84 hours.

The world's loudest drummer is Frenchman Jéróme Dehèdin, who has been known to reach a volume of 109 **decibels**. That is as loud as a propeller plane taking off.

What are drums made of?

Drum shells can be made of almost any material. Traditional drums are often made of carved or hollowed-out wood. Modern drums can be made out of anything, from specially treated wood to plastic and even metal. Different materials create different sounds.

Drum heads can also be made from different materials. In the past, animal skins were used, and this is still sometimes the case with traditional instruments. Modern drum sets use a plastic called Mylar. Marching band drums are made of another type of plastic, called Kevlar.

Tuning the drums

A drum is **tuned** using **tension rods**. These steel pins or wooden pegs hold the head in place across the top of the shell. They screw into little plugs, known as lugs, around the side of the drum. The tension rods tighten a metal ring called the counter hoop. The hoop pulls down on the head and stretches it across the top of the shell. Tightening or loosening the tension rods tunes the drum until it gives the desired sound.

A single drum is made up of many different parts.

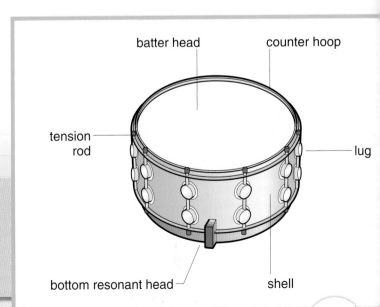

batter head

counter hoop

tension rod

lug

bottom resonant head

shell

Which Musical Family Are Drums From?

Drums are **percussion instruments**. A percussion instrument is any instrument that is hit to produce a sound. Other percussion instruments are the triangle and xylophone.

Cymbals

Cymbals are percussion instruments, too, and are used with most drum sets. As a drummer, you will also need to learn how to play the cymbals correctly.

Cymbals are made from copper mixed with tin and silver. They can be made by hand or machine. Look closely at a cymbal and you will see rings of marks where the metal has been beaten. The marks affect its sound.

There are three other things that affect a cymbal's sound: its size, its thickness, and the amount of copper, tin, and silver it contains. A cymbal's sound is also affected by how hard you hit it and the type of **beater** you hit it with.

Drummers in rock bands often have several kinds of cymbals on their drum set.

This drummer is playing his hi-hats and snare drum.

Types of cymbal

Hi-hats are actually a pair of cymbals mounted on a stand that has a pedal. The two hi-hats are brought against each other by using the pedal. They are held in place with a clutch. The hi-hat is mainly used as an **accompaniment** to the **snare drum** and **bass drum**.

Crash cymbals come in many different shapes and sizes. They are used to provide **accents** to the **rhythm** and in **drum fills**. Some crash cymbals have up-turned sides. These are called china-crash cymbals, and they are extremely loud. A smaller, quieter type of crash cymbal is known as a splash cymbal.

Ride cymbals are the heaviest type of cymbal. They are sometimes used instead of the hi-hat to accompany the snare and bass drums. When played lightly they have a very delicate sound, but when played heavily they are even louder than crash cymbals.

Percussion instruments from around the world

There are many different percussion instruments played around the world. Some are drums, but others are not. They are all played by striking them with a hand or a beater.

Drummers in India play the tabla. The tabla are two short, upright drums, one smaller than the other. They are played with the fingers and the palms of the hands. Over twenty sounds can be made with a single tabla, depending on where and how you hit it. This is far more than most Western drums.

The small drum in the tabla set is called the dayan (which means "right"). It is usually made of wood and is played with the right hand. The larger drum is called the bayan (meaning "left"). This is usually made of copper.

DRUM FACTS: Did you know?

The word *tabla* comes from the Arabic word *tabl*, meaning "drum."

In India, the tabla is the most popular percussion instrument.

Traditional Japanese drums are called taiko, meaning "large drum." A taiko drum consists of two pieces of cowhide stretched over a large wooden body. Traditionally, the body of a taiko drum is carved from a single piece of wood. Taiko drums are **tuned** using ropes, which stretch the cowhide over the body of the drum.

Taiko drums range in size from being small and easy to carry to being very large. The size determines how a taiko drum is played. Large taiko drums are placed on their sides, like a bass drum. The player beats the drum with wooden mallets.

In Japan's history, taiko drums were used by priests to chase spirits from rice fields, and soldiers used them to frighten their enemies. Today, taiko drums are used in theatrical displays. There are many percussion groups in Japan that use them.

Some percussion instruments, like this xylophone, can be used to play a tune.

Steel drums are unlike many other drums because they can be used to play a tune. Originally, they were made from old oil drums (containers). The sides were cut off and the base was beaten until it formed a shallow bowl. Sections of the bowl were then beaten again, until each area played a different note when struck.

Today, steel drums are professionally made, although the basic design has not changed. They are played with rubber beaters to produce a distinctively soft sound. They are used by groups called steel bands to play Caribbean music styles such as **calypso**.

Other percussion instruments

There are many other types of percussion instruments you can use to create a rhythm. Tambourines, woodblocks, cowbells, triangles, and maracas each make a different sound.

The sound of the steel drum instantly gives music a unique sound.

DRUM FACTS: The largest drum

The world's largest drum is the Ireland Millennium Drum. It is 15 feet, 6 inches (4.7 meters) across and 6 feet, 3 inches (1.9 meters) deep. It was first played in Dublin, as part of Ireland's Millennium Festivals.

What Types of Music Can You Play with the Drums?

There really is no limit to the sorts of music that you can play with the drums. They are used in virtually every style of music, from **classical** and **jazz** to **samba**, R&B, and rock. A drummer can play in a band where he or she will need lots of **amplification** or in a small **acoustic** group where he or she will need to play as quietly as possible.

 Rock music is just one of the many styles of music that you can play using the drums.

Drums are used in classical music. Timpani can be used to provide dramatic accents to a piece of music.

The role of the drum

In most music, drums are used to create **rhythm**. In rock music, for instance, the drummer **accompanies** the other musicians. In classical music, however, drums are used either to create a rhythm or to provide **accents**. Instruments such as the **timpani** are used to draw attention to certain parts or characters. In the musical story *Peter and the Wolf*, timpani are used to represent the hunter.

Drums can also be played together, in **ensembles**. Both the Japanese taiko drum and the Caribbean steel drum are usually played in groups. If you have friends who play **percussion instruments**, you could form your own group.

Getting started

When you first start playing the drums, you will probably play in a school orchestra, marching band, or concert band. These are all especially good places to learn how to play the drums. You may begin by learning to play other percussion instruments. Most school orchestras will lend you an instrument to play so you do not have to buy your own. You will also receive instructions on how to play it correctly. Getting a band together with friends can also be fun, since you will be able to play the sorts of music that you are most interested in.

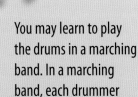

You may learn to play the drums in a marching band. In a marching band, each drummer plays a separate drum.

PROTECT YOUR EARS!

Drums can be very loud, and the sound can harm your ears. Wherever you play, you should never play without wearing earplugs. Earplugs can be bought from any drugstore. They do not actually block out all of the sound, just the parts of the sound that are harmful to your ears.

Who Plays the Drums?

In all styles of music, there are some musicians who stand out. Many drummers from different backgrounds have become famous for being excellent musicians. Their playing inspires and entertains people.

Mitch Mitchell

Mitch Mitchell was one of the most influential drummers of the 1960s and 1970s. He is most famous for playing with The Jimi Hendrix Experience. Mitchell began his career as a **jazz** drummer. Playing with Hendrix meant that he had to be very good at **improvisation**, especially when playing live, since Hendrix was known to improvise on stage. Mitchell was one of Hendrix's most important partners.

Mitch's drumming blended jazz and rock styles. His style of playing was unknown in the 1960s, since drums had always been expected to stay in the background. He is now retired and lives in Europe.

Rick Allen of Def Leppard is well known for customizing his drum set to cater to the fact that he only has one arm.

Buddy Rich

Buddy Rich is regarded as the greatest jazz drummer of all time. His career started when he was eighteen and spanned decades.

Buddy performed with many jazz bands, playing with other famous jazz musicians such as Dizzy Gillespie and Louis Armstrong. He toured the world and played for presidents John F. Kennedy and Franklin D. Roosevelt and for the British queen.

He won many awards for his drumming, despite the fact that he never received a single drumming lesson and refused to practice between performances.

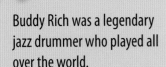

Buddy Rich was a legendary jazz drummer who played all over the world.

Ahmir "Questlove" Thompson

Ahmir Thompson was born in 1971. He is best known for his work with the band The Roots. He began drumming at the age of two, and by age seven he was performing on stage. After graduating from the Philadelphia High School for Performing Arts, he formed The Roots. The band released their first record in 1993. Ahmir's style is very experimental and is influenced by hip-hop.

Manu Katche

Manu Katche is considered to be one of today's leading drummers. He is a session drummer. A session musician does not belong to any particular band, but performs and records with many different artists. Manu can be heard on records by Peter Gabriel and Youssou N'Dour, among others. A session drummer has to be very good at playing different styles of music. They may play rock music one day and **funk** or jazz the next.

Manu Katche blends traditional rock sounds with drumming techniques from Africa and Europe.

Evelyn Glennie

Evelyn Glennie was born in 1965 in Scotland. She is a **solo classical** percussionist and studied at London's Royal Academy of Music. She performs with a wide variety of orchestras and musicians and plays over 100 concerts a year.

Evelyn has been deaf since the age of twelve. This does not **inhibit** her ability to play the drums or perform. She is able to tell the **pitch** of a note by feeling the **vibrations** it makes through her feet and legs.

How Would I Learn to Play the Drums?

You might try to learn the drums yourself, or you could take lessons. Either way, practice will help you to improve and become more confident.

Learning the basics

If you take lessons, you will probably not start off with a five-piece drum set. Instead, you will likely begin by learning the individual instruments that are played in a school orchestra, marching band, or concert band, such as the **snare drum**, **bass drum**, and cymbals. You might also try mallet instruments, such as the xylophone and marimba, as well as other **percussion instruments**, such as the woodblock, maracas, or tambourine.

It is a good idea to visit a music store, both for the percussion instruments on sale and also for details about teachers and other musicians who might be looking for someone to play with.

When you start on a drum set, you will need to learn a few basic **rhythms**. A music teacher can show you these. A teacher will also show you how to hold the sticks correctly and how to sit when you play.

You can also try teaching yourself. You can get a feel for the basics of drumming just by listening to other drummers. Put on your favorite music and listen carefully to what the drummer is doing. What rhythm is he or she playing? How does the drummer draw attention to parts of the song—is it with **drum fills** and cymbal hits? What else does he or she do? Do any other drummers do this?

Drummers use diagrams to illustrate how their set is assembled.

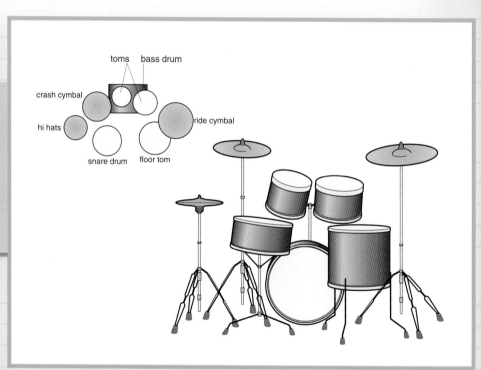

DRUM FACTS: Largest drum set

The world's largest drum set is played by Michael McNeil from Missouri. His drum set consists of 105 pieces: 7 bass drums, 19 toms, 3 snares, 4 **electronic drums**, 10 other drums, 25 cymbals, 16 bells, 20 other percussion instruments, and 1 kitchen sink.

Your first exercise

Most drummers will tell you that they always tap on things. This is, after all, how drumming started many thousands of years ago. Before long, recognizing rhythms will become a habit. This first exercise will get you thinking about those rhythms.

- First of all, with your right hand, tap four times on any surface in front of you. One ... Two ... Three ... Four. (You will usually use your right hand to play a **hi-hat** or a **ride cymbal**.)

Playing the drums in a band or orchestra is a fun way to practice and to learn how to play with others.

- Now, do it again, but this time add a tap with your right foot on the counts of one and two. (You will use your right foot to play the bass drum.)

- Next, add a tap with your left hand on the count of three. (You will use your left hand to play the snare drum.)

Work slowly until you get the hang of it. Keep it steady until you can play it from memory and you no longer have to count along.

And that's it: you have just learned a simple rock drum beat! This beat is called Eighth Rock 4/4. Most rock music uses this basic beat. It might be hidden or hard to recognize, but it will be there if you listen closely.

Recordings to Listen To

Classical

Sergei Prokofiev, *Peter and the Wolf* (Naxos, 1998). This piece of **classical** music features a section that is almost entirely played on the **timpani**. Each character in the story is represented by a different instrument. The timpani are used for the part of the hunter.

Richard Strauss, *Also Sprach Zarathustra* (Deutsche Grammophon, 1996). This piece is very famous and can be heard in the movie *2001: A Space Odyssey*. It has lots of timpani in it.

Jazz

Big Swing Face (Blue Note, 1996). A CD of **jazz** music featuring Buddy Rich on drums.
Watts at Scott's (Sanctuary, 2004). A recording of a ten-piece band playing jazz classics, featuring the Rolling Stones' Charlie Watts on drums.

Rock

The Foo Fighters, *The Colour and the Shape* (RCA, 1997). The Foo Fighters are an important U.S. rock band. Their drummer, Taylor Hawkins, has perfected the rock sound.

Peter Gabriel, *So* (Geffen, 2002). Manu Katche plays the drums on this album. It is worth listening to his African-influenced **rhythms**.

Jimi Hendrix, *Experience Hendrix: The Best of Jimi Hendrix* (MCA, 1998). This CD features the drumming of Mitch Mitchell.

The Police, *Synchronicity* (A&M, 1983). The Police were an pop/rock band. Their drummer, Stewart Copeland, used **funk** and reggae styles.

The Who, *The Ultimate Collection* (MCA, 2002). The Who are a rock band. They had a very energetic drummer named Keith Moon, who was famous for his **drum fills**.

World music

Bhai Gaitonde, *Tabla* (India Archives, 1999). This features music performed on the tabla.
Sand & Steel (Trojan, 2005). Steel drumming by a wide variety of Caribbean steel bands.
Wadaiko Matsuriza, *Japanese Drums* (Arc, 2003). This features music performed on Japanese drums (taiko drums).

Timeline of Drum History

6000 B.C.E.   The oldest drums that have been found come from this time

3000 B.C.E.   Taiko drums arrive in Japan from China

204 B.C.E.   Greeks and Romans discover African drums

1500s   African slaves and their drums taken to the Americas

mid-1600s   Earliest form of **snare drum** invented

1800s   Invention of the tabla

late 1800s to 1930s   The modern drum set takes shape

1917   Buddy Rich born

1936   Composer Sergei Prokofiev commissioned by the Central Children's Theater to produce a piece that will introduce children to the instruments of the orchestra. The result is the musical story *Peter and the Wolf*.

around 1939   Steel drum invented in Trinidad

1950s   Rock and roll music begins to develop. Drum patterns and rhythms become more complex. The drum set begins to expand.

1965   Evelyn Glennie born

1966   Mitch Mitchell joins The Jimi Hendrix Experience

1980s   **Electronic drums** are introduced

1999   Ireland's Millennium Drum, the world's largest drum, is designed and constructed by Brian Fleming and Paraic Breathnac

2004   Arulanantham Suresh Joachim of Australia completes the longest-ever drum marathon, playing for 84 hours

Glossary

accent stress or emphasis

accompany play along with

acoustic played without being made louder electronically

amplify make louder, using electronic circuits

bass drum largest drum in the set. This drum has the deepest tone and is played with a pedal.

beater tool used to hit a drum

calypso Caribbean song with a changing rhythm and usually improvised words

classical formal style of music usually written for orchestral instruments

crash cymbal main type of cymbal used with drum sets

decibel unit used to measure sound

drum fill phrase that can be played to link parts of a rhythm together

electronic drums pads with built-in electronic sensors that respond when hit

ensemble group of musicians performing together

funk type of music with a strong beat, similar to jazz music

head part of the drum that is struck

hi-hat two cymbals of equal size mounted above one another on a stand fitted with a pedal

improvise make up music as it is played

inhibit prevent from doing something

jazz type of music that developed in the 20th century in the United States

membrane thin, flexible skin

modify adapt or make changes

percussion instrument any instrument that is struck to play a note. Drums are percussion instruments, as are xylophones, triangles, and bells.

pitch specific note that a drum is tuned to play

rhythm beat of a song. A drummer plays a rhythm.

ride cymbal largest and heaviest type of cymbal

roll skilled drum technique, used to create an almost continuous sound

samba ballroom dance from Brazil

shell body of a drum

snare drum one of the main drums in a drum set. Its name and sound come from the steel springs that lie flat against the bottom.

solo play an instrument without accompaniment

tension rods steel rods used to alter the tension in the head and the sound of the drum

timpani large, bowl-shaped drum used in classical music

tune alter the sound of a drum by adjusting the tension rods

vibration movement to and from

Further Resources

Books

Berry, Mick, and Jason Gianni. *The Drummer's Bible: How to Play Every Drum Style from Afro-Cuban to Zydeco.* Tucson, Ariz.: See Sharp, 2004.

Blades, James, and Johnny Dean. *How to Play Drums: Everything You Need to Know to Play the Drums.* New York: St. Martin's Griffin, 2002.

Harris, Pamela K. *Drums.* Chanhassen, Minn.: Child's World, 2000.

Kallen, Stuart A. *The Instruments of Music.* San Diego: Lucent, 2003.

O'Brien, Eileen. *Learn to Play the Drums.* Tulsa, Okla.: EDC, 1999.

DVDs

African Drumming (Wea Corp, 2005)

Legends of Jazz Drumming, Vols. 1 & 2 (Warner Bros, 2005)

The Police: Synchronicity Concert (A&M, 2005)

Websites

http://www.playmusic.org
This website offers facts about orchestral instruments and introduces you to professional musicians. It also lets you create your own musical compositions and helps you find teachers and orchestras in your area.

http://www.music.vt.edu/musicdictionary/textp/Percussioninstruments.html
This encyclopedia features different percussion instruments from different countries.

http://www.drummerworld.com
This website contains biographical information about many rock and jazz drummers.

Index